A Kalmus Classic Edition

Nikolaus
BRUHNS

THREE PRELUDES

FOR ORGAN

K 04101

1. Praeludium.

4
Adagio. (♩=56)
Con moto (♩.=69)
12/8
stringendo
Adagio. (♩=56)
tr
rall.
Tempo ordinario. (♩=80)
tr
pl.
tr
tr

Adagio
tr long
Cantabile. (♩. 96)
rall.
p
rit.
Presto. (♪ =126)
Harpeggio

poco rit.
Grave. (♩ = 72)
Presto (♩ = 112)
Adagio (♪ = 76)
tr
Allegro. (♩. = 72)

p
pp rallent.
24/16
Presto. (♪. = 100)
24/16
l.
rit. poco a poco
tr

2. Praeludium.

poco rit.
tr
Tempo ordinario (♩. = 76)

Piu mosso (♩ = 84)
tr
tr
l.
r

Allegro. (♩ = 88)
tr
l.
l.

Moderato. (♩ = 84)
allargando
tr
tr
tr
tr

3. Praeludium.

Presto. (♩. = 112)
Org.
Echo
Echo
Echo
Echo

Adagio. (♪=92)
Vivace (♩=144)
tr
tr
l.

tr
tr
rallent.
l.
p
pp
Adagio. (♩=92)
tr
tr
Allegro (♩=100)

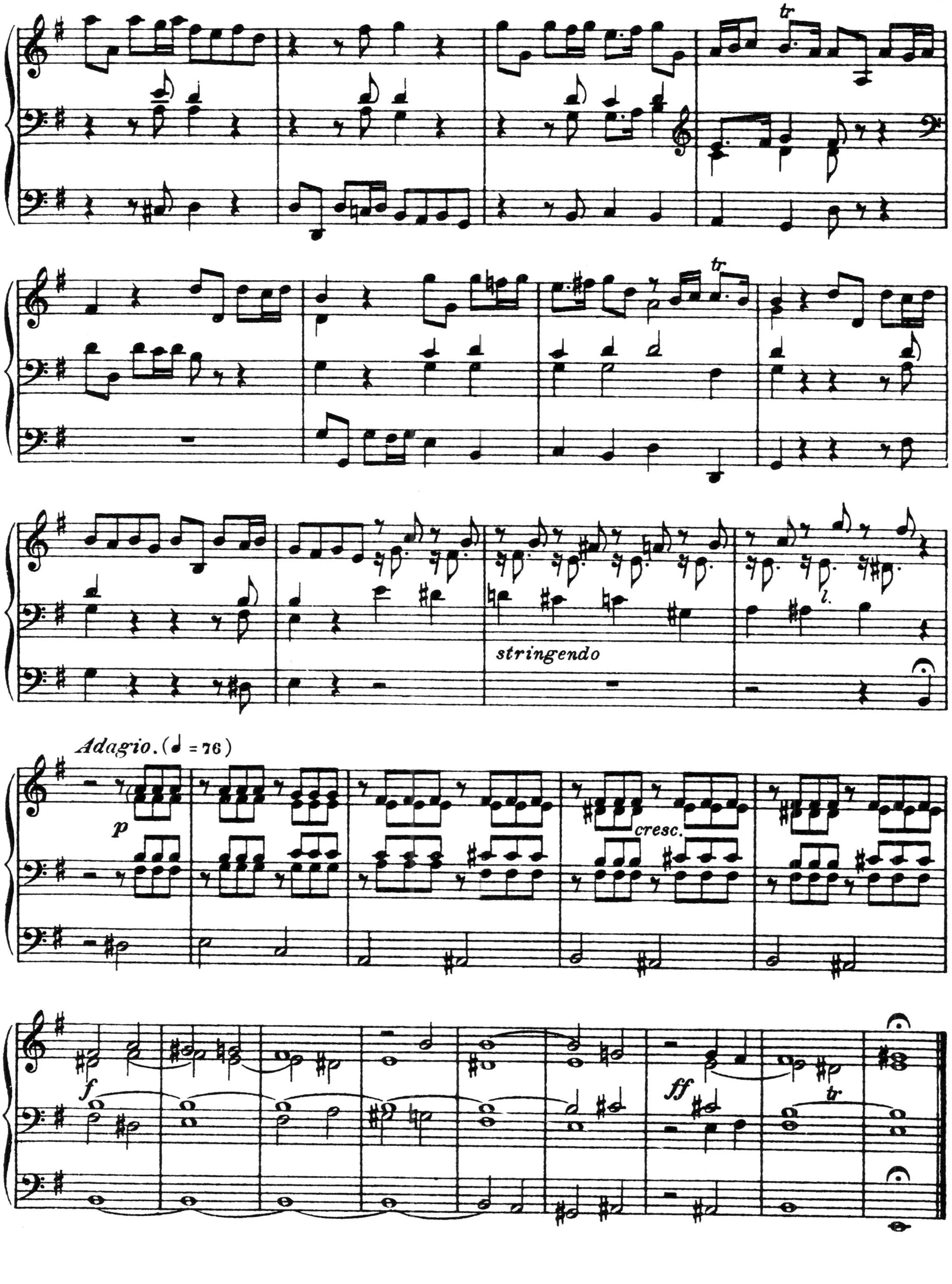
tr
tr
stringendo
l.
Adagio. (♩ = 76)
p
cresc.
f
ff
tr